The Solar System

Robin Birch

Mercury

CHELSEA CLUBHOUSE
An Imprint of Chelsea House Publishers
A Haights Cross Communications Company
Philadelphia

This edition first published in 2004 in the United States of America by Chelsea Clubhouse, a division of Chelsea House Publishers and a subsidiary of Haights Cross Communications.

Chelsea House Publishers
1974 Sproul Road, Suite 400
Broomall, PA 19008-0914

The Chelsea House world wide web address is www.chelseahouse.com

Library of Congress Cataloging-in-Publication Data Applied for.
ISBN 0-7910-7928-7

First published in 2004 by
MACMILLAN EDUCATION AUSTRALIA PTY LTD
627 Chapel Street, South Yarra, Australia, 3141

Associated companies and representatives throughout the world.

Edited by Anna Fern
Text and cover design by Cristina Neri, Canary Design
Illustrations by Melissa Webb
Photo research by Legend Images

Printed in China

Acknowledgements
The author and publisher are grateful to the following for permission to reproduce copyright material:

Cover photograph of Mercury courtesy of Photodisc.

TSADO/NASA/Tom Stack/Auscape, p. 29; Australian Picture Library/Corbis, pp. 5 (left), 26; Getty Images/Taxi, p. 13; Calvin J. Hamilton, pp. 7, 11 (right); Walter Myers/www.arcadiastreet.com, pp. 10, 18; NASA/JPL, pp. 5 (right), 14 (bottom left); NASA/JPL/Northwestern University, p. 17 (both); NASA/NSSDC, pp. 14 (bottom right), 23, 25 (both); Photodisc, pp. 11 (left), 20; Photolibrary.com, p. 12; Photolibrary.com/SPL, pp. 4 (bottom right), 6, 15, 16, 21, 24, 27, 28.

Background and border images, including view of Mercury, courtesy of Photodisc.

While every care has been taken to trace and acknowledge copyright, the publisher tenders their apologies for any accidental infringement where copyright has proved untraceable. Where the attempt has been unsuccessful, the publisher welcomes information that would redress the situation.

Please note
At the time of printing, the Internet addresses appearing in this book were correct. Owing to the dynamic nature of the Internet, however, we cannot guarantee that all these addresses will remain correct.

Contents

Discovering Mercury   4

The First Planet   6

On Mercury   8

Surface Features   14

Exploring Mercury   24

Mercury Fact Summary   30

Glossary   31

Index   32

Glossary words

When you see a word printed in bold, **like this**, you can look up its meaning in the glossary on page 31.

Discovering Mercury

Mercury is a **planet** which looks like a bright **star**. People have seen Mercury in the sky since **ancient** times. Mercury is always fairly close to the Sun in the sky. Sometimes Mercury can be seen low in the western sky, just after sunset. Sometimes it can be seen low in the eastern sky, just before sunrise. During the day, the Sun's light is so bright that we cannot see Mercury.

▼ Mercury in the sky at sunset

It is dangerous to look for Mercury while the Sun is in the sky. The Sun burns your eyes if you look at it.

▲ This is the symbol for Mercury.

Mercury

The ancient Greeks called Mercury "Apollo" when they saw it in the morning and "Hermes" when they saw it in the evening. In Greek myths, Apollo was the god of light and Hermes was the messenger of the gods.

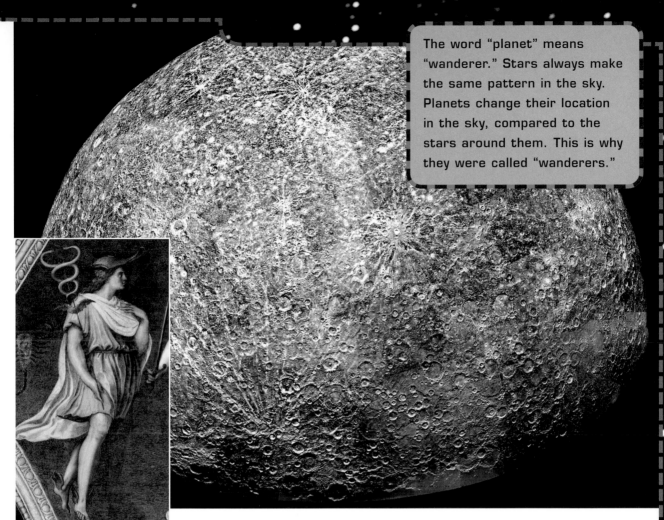

The word "planet" means "wanderer." Stars always make the same pattern in the sky. Planets change their location in the sky, compared to the stars around them. This is why they were called "wanderers."

▲ The Roman god Mercury

▲ This photo of Mercury was taken by the *Mariner 10* space probe.

Mercury is named after the Roman god Mercury, who was a fast-moving messenger with wings on his heels. The planet Mercury was probably given this name because it moves swiftly through the sky.

The **space probe** *Mariner 10* visited Mercury in 1974 and 1975 and took thousands of photographs of Mercury as it flew past. This was the first time close-up photographs of Mercury had been taken. There have been no other close-up photographs taken since then and no other spacecraft has visited Mercury.

The First Planet

Mercury is part of the solar system, which consists mainly of the Sun and nine planets. The planets **revolve** around the Sun. Mercury is the closest planet to the Sun.

The solar system also has comets and asteroids moving around in it. Comets are large balls of rock, ice, **gas**, and dust which **orbit** the Sun. Comets start their orbit far away from the Sun. They travel in close to the Sun, go around it, and then travel out again. When they come close to the Sun, comets grow a tail.

Asteroids are rocks. There are millions of asteroids in the solar system. They can be small or large. The largest asteroid, named Ceres, is about 584 miles (940 kilometers) across. Most asteroids orbit the Sun in a path called the asteroid belt, between the orbits of Mars and Jupiter.

▶ The solar system

The solar system is about 4,600 million years old.

The planets in the solar system are made of rock, ice, gas, and liquid. Mercury, Venus, Earth, and Mars are made of rock. Pluto is probably made of rock and ice. These are the smallest planets.

Jupiter, Saturn, Uranus, and Neptune are made mainly of gas and liquid. They are the largest planets. They are often called the gas giants, because they have no solid ground to land on.

Planets, comets, and asteroids are lit up by light from the Sun. They do not make their own light the way stars do.

► The planets, from smallest to largest, are: Pluto, Mercury, Mars, Venus, Earth, Neptune, Uranus, Saturn, and Jupiter.

Planet	Average distance from Sun	
Mercury	35,960,000 miles	(57,910,000 kilometers)
Venus	67,190,000 miles	(108,200,000 kilometers)
Earth	92,900,000 miles	(149,600,000 kilometers)
Mars	141,550,000 miles	(227,940,000 kilometers)
Jupiter	483,340,000 miles	(778,330,000 kilometers)
Saturn	887,660,000 miles	(1,429,400,000 kilometers)
Uranus	1,782,880,000 miles	(2,870,990,000 kilometers)
Neptune	2,796,000,000 miles	(4,504,000,000 kilometers)
Pluto	3,672,300,000 miles	(5,913,520,000 kilometers)

The name "solar system" comes from the word "Solaris." This is the official name for the Sun. The Sun is a star.

On Mercury

As it travels around the Sun, the rocky planet Mercury spins on its **axis**.

Revolution

Mercury revolves around the Sun in an elliptical or oval-shaped orbit. When it is closest to the Sun, Mercury is 29 million miles (46 million kilometers) from the Sun. When it is furthest away, Mercury is 43 million miles (70 million kilometers) from the Sun.

Mercury travels about 30 miles (50 kilometers) every second, which is faster than any of the other planets. Mercury takes 88 Earth days to orbit the Sun once. This is the length of Mercury's year. The Sun's **gravity** keeps Mercury circling around it.

Many years ago, people were searching for another planet, even closer to the Sun than Mercury. They called it Vulcan. Today we know that Vulcan does not exist.

Ancient people believed that Mercury and the Sun circled around Earth.

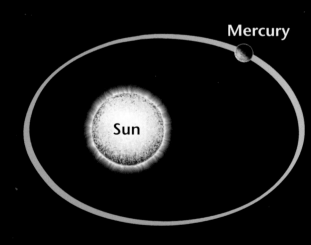

▲ The orbit of Mercury

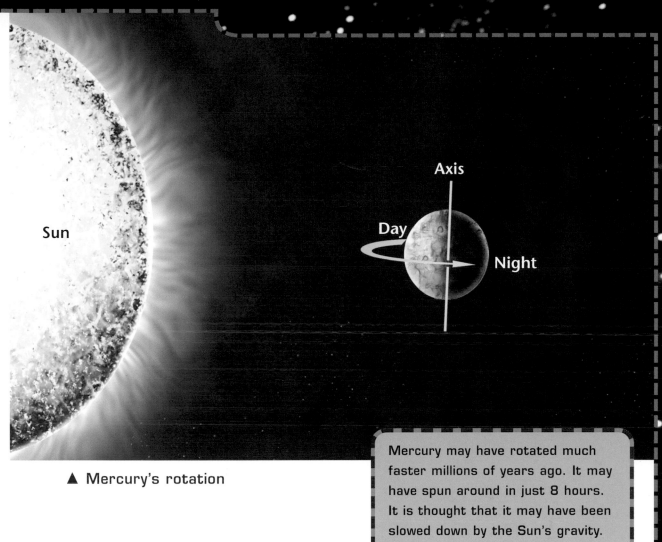

Sun

Axis

Day

Night

▲ Mercury's rotation

Mercury may have rotated much faster millions of years ago. It may have spun around in just 8 hours. It is thought that it may have been slowed down by the Sun's gravity.

Rotation

Mercury **rotates** on its axis, in an upright position, taking 58.65 Earth days to spin around once. Mercury rotates one-and-a-half times each time it circles the Sun. A day on Mercury, from sunrise to sunrise, lasts for 176 Earth days.

If a person could live on Mercury, the day would seem very strange. From some places on Mercury, they would see the Sun rise, and appear to grow larger. Then the Sun might go back down again, becoming smaller, before coming up again. These effects are because of Mercury's slow rotation and elliptical orbit.

Size and Structure

Mercury is 3,030 miles (4,880 kilometers) in **diameter**. It is smaller than Earth and only a little larger than Earth's Moon. Mercury is made up of a **core**, a **mantle**, and a **crust**.

Mercury's core takes up a large part of the inside of the planet. It is made of about 65 percent iron and is probably partly molten, or liquid. The core is about 2,200 to 2,400 miles (3,600 to 3,800 kilometers) in diameter.

The mantle and crust are made of rocks and soils similar to Earth's. The mantle and crust together are only about 300 to 400 miles (500 to 600 kilometers) thick.

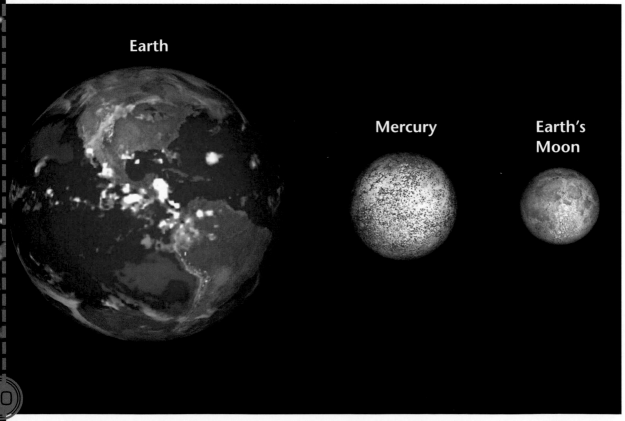

Earth

Mercury

Earth's Moon

▲ Compare the size of Mercury to Earth and Earth's Moon.

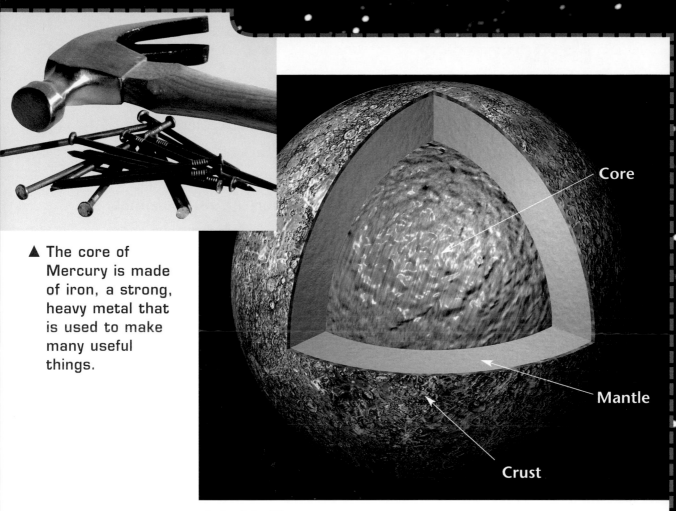

▲ The core of Mercury is made of iron, a strong, heavy metal that is used to make many useful things.

Core

Mantle

Crust

▲ Inside Mercury

Mercury's large, heavy iron core gives the planet a high **density**. This means that Mercury is heavy for its size. Earth is the densest planet in the solar system. Mercury is the second densest planet—it is nearly as dense as Earth.

Magnetic Field

Mercury's iron core gives the planet a weak magnetic field. Planets with magnetic fields are huge magnets. Earth has a strong magnetic field. A compass needle is a magnet which lines itself up with Earth's magnetic field.

Atmosphere

Mercury has a very thin **atmosphere**—so thin that it is hardly there. (In comparison, Earth has a thick atmosphere made of air and water drops.) Mercury's atmosphere is made of gases which have been blasted off the planet's surface by **solar wind** from the Sun. These gases do not stay near Mercury for long, but escape into space. This is because the Sun's heat makes them move so fast that they escape from Mercury's gravity.

As there is almost no atmosphere on Mercury, there is no wind or rain to wear away the surface. This is one of the reasons why Mercury has changed very little for millions of years.

◀ The Sun above Mercury. The sky on Mercury looks black because there is almost no atmosphere.

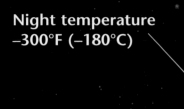

Night temperature
−300°F (−180°C)

Day temperature
680°F (360°C)

The temperature on Mercury ranges between 680 degrees Fahrenheit (360 degrees Celsius) during the day and −300 degrees Fahrenheit (−180 degrees Celsius) during the night.

▲ Day and night on Mercury

Temperature

Mercury gets very hot during the day and very cold during the night. One reason for the temperature difference is that Mercury's days and nights are very long. A day followed by a night on Mercury lasts 176 Earth days. The Sun blasts down during the long day, scorching the ground. Then the Sun sets for the long night, and the ground becomes very cold.

Another reason for the temperature difference is that Mercury does not have enough atmosphere to act as a blanket to keep it warm during the night. If Mercury had a thicker atmosphere, then the day and night temperatures would not be so different from each other.

Surface Features

The surface of Mercury has **craters** and holes, long ridges and wrinkles, and flat plains.

Craters

Mercury looks like Earth's Moon. Both are gray and are covered with craters. They both have a rocky surface covered with thick dust.

Mercury and Earth's Moon were bombarded heavily with asteroids when they were young, around 4,000 million years ago. This was when there were many asteroids flying around in the young solar system. The smallest asteroids can be as small as a pebble, and the largest asteroids can be hundreds of miles across. When large asteroids hit planets or **moons**, they make a crater, and rock and dust fly up from the surface.

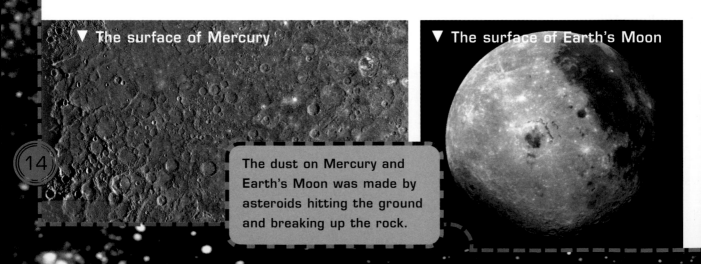

▼ The surface of Mercury

▼ The surface of Earth's Moon

The dust on Mercury and Earth's Moon was made by asteroids hitting the ground and breaking up the rock.

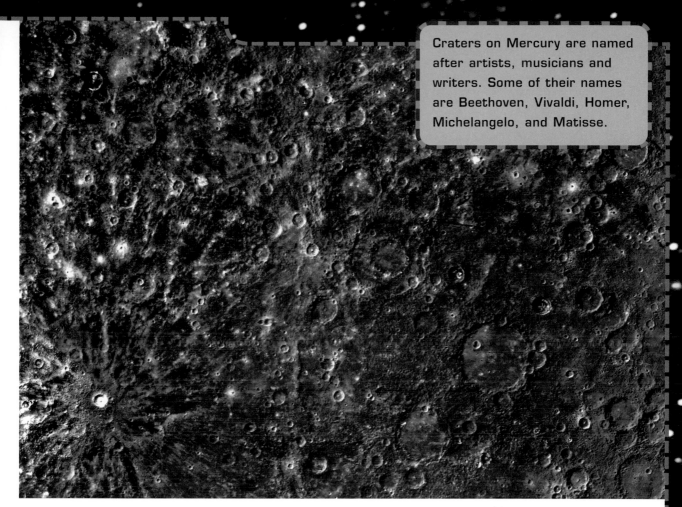

Craters on Mercury are named after artists, musicians and writers. Some of their names are Beethoven, Vivaldi, Homer, Michelangelo, and Matisse.

▲ Craters on Mercury

The smallest craters detected on Mercury are 300 feet (100 meters) across. The largest crater detected is 800 miles (1,300 kilometers) across. Some craters are young, with sharp edges. Older craters have smooth edges because asteroids have been hitting them over the years.

Mercury and Earth's Moon have almost no atmosphere and no liquid water, so there has been no wind or water to wash away old craters. The Moon has had some **lava** flowing on its surface, and Mercury has had a smaller amount of lava. However, there has not been enough lava to cover up very many craters on Mercury or on the Moon.

Rayed Craters

Some craters on Mercury have rays coming out of them. The rays are lines which spread out from the crater, like spokes on a wheel. The rays are paler in color than the other ground, so are easy to see. They are made of light-colored dust which was thrown up when a rock hit Mercury, making the crater. When the dust settled, it formed into rays.

The rays can sometimes be hundreds of miles long. Some craters on Earth's Moon also have rays. Rayed craters sometimes have circles of bright dust around the crater, called halos.

▼ Rayed craters on Mercury with bright halos

If the rays are not covered up by anything else, it can mean that the crater is young.

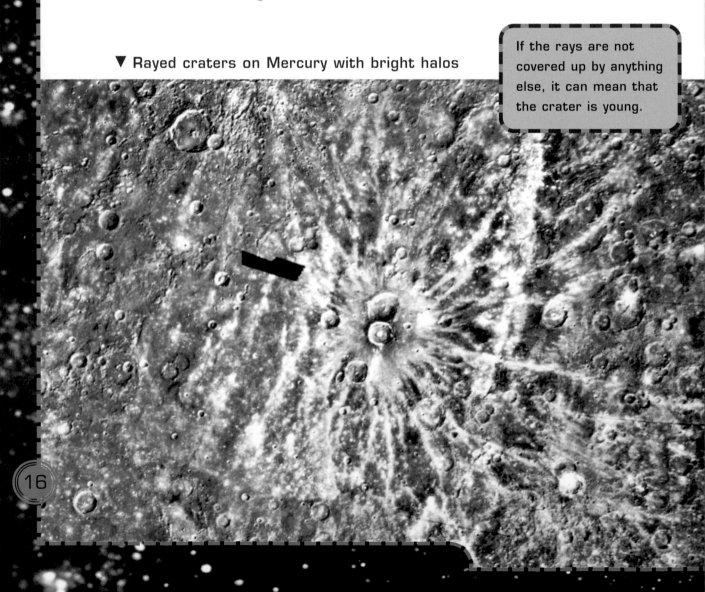

16

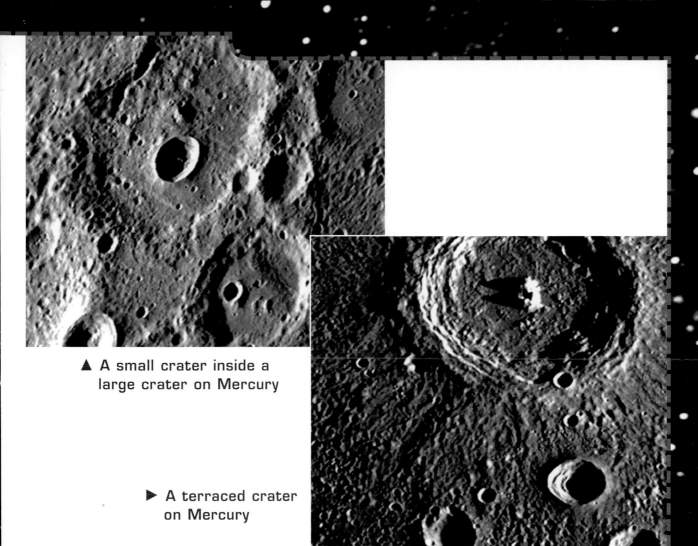

▲ A small crater inside a
large crater on Mercury

► A terraced crater
on Mercury

Craters inside Craters

In some places on Mercury, there are small craters inside larger
craters. This is where an asteroid has hit an old crater and
made a new crater inside the old one.

Terraced Craters

Some of Mercury's larger craters are terraced, which means the
inside walls of the craters do not slope down smoothly.
Instead, the crater walls have different levels, like steps. These
craters have a flat floor, often with a mountain in the middle.

Ridges

Mercury's surface has wrinkles on it which make long ridges. Sometimes they are hundreds of miles long, and can be 2 miles (3 kilometers) high. These wrinkles could also be called scarps or cliffs, and there are similar long ridges on Earth. The ridges on Mercury were probably caused by the crust shrinking as it cooled, when the planet was young.

Some ridges cut through crater rings, which shows they were formed after the crater had been made. The land on either side of the ridge squeezed together, pushing the ridge up.

▼ Discovery Scarp, on Mercury

Ice

▲ An artist's impression of ice inside a deep crater on Mercury

Ice on Mercury

Astronomers have discovered there may be some ice, or frozen water, on Mercury. It could have come from icy comets crashing into Mercury. This ice may be deep inside some craters at the north **pole** of Mercury. The Sun never shines into these craters, because Mercury rotates in an upright position. The craters stay very cold, at a temperature of about –260 degrees Fahrenheit (–160 degrees Celsius), which means that if the ice is there, it would never melt.

In 1974 and 1975, the only the space probe to visit Mercury, *Mariner 10*, did not visit or photograph Mercury's north pole. The discovery of the possibility of ice at the north pole was made later, in 1991, using radar to observe Mercury from Earth.

Plains

Mercury has a few fairly flat areas on it, called plains. Some plains were formed from the dust which settled after an asteroid hit Mercury. Other plains were formed by lava flowing over the surface. The hot, molten rock came from under the surface of Mercury and covered up or filled craters in the area. These lava flows happened while Mercury was still young.

▼ A lava flow on Earth. The liquid rock will cool and become a hard, rocky plain.

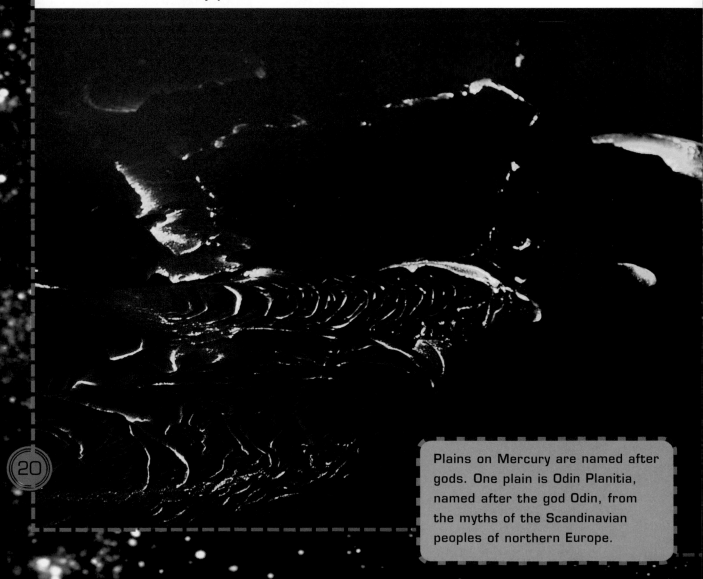

Plains on Mercury are named after gods. One plain is Odin Planitia, named after the god Odin, from the myths of the Scandinavian peoples of northern Europe.

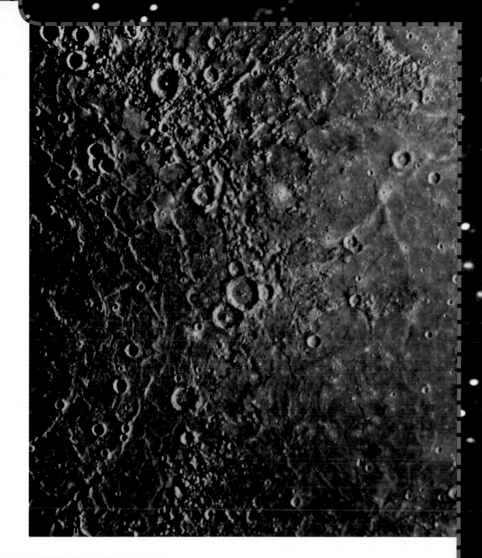

► A smooth plain on Mercury

There are not many plains on Mercury because it has a hard, thick crust. The crust has stopped lava getting through it from the mantle below.

When Mercury was a young planet, about 4,000 million years ago, lava sometimes flowed onto its surface. At this time, many rocks were hitting Mercury, making craters. For the next 500 million years or so, Mercury cooled down. As it cooled, the crust shrank and became very hard and strong. After that, lava could not escape onto the surface, which is why there have been no more flat plains made in the last 3,500 million years.

Caloris Basin

Caloris Basin is a huge bowl-shaped hole on the surface of Mercury, measuring 800 miles (1,300 kilometers) across. It was made by an enormous asteroid which crashed into Mercury 4,000 million years ago. Rocks and dust were thrown as far as 500 miles (800 kilometers) across the planet. The asteroid, which was probably about 90 miles (150 kilometers) across, would have smashed into pieces.

Caloris Basin is surrounded by rings of mountains up to 2 miles (3 kilometers) high called the Caloris Montes. The rings of mountains formed like the ripples which spread out when a pebble is thrown into water. The basin is covered with smaller craters, made when more asteroids hit the area. Caloris Basin also has cracks and ridges on it.

▼ An artist's impression of Caloris Basin on Mercury

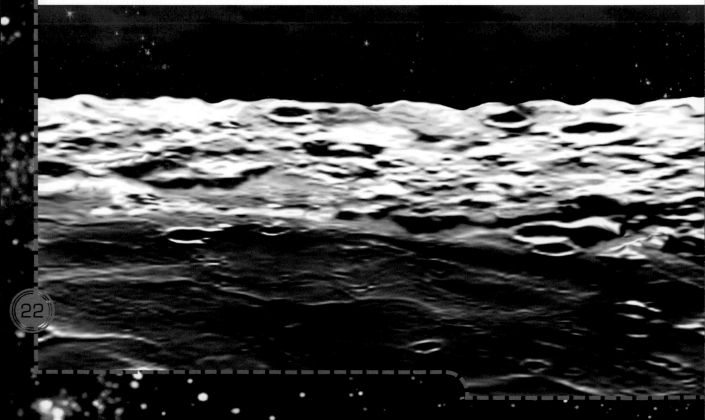

▲ Weird terrain on Mercury opposite the Caloris Basin

The word "*caloris*" is Latin for "heat." The Caloris Basin has this name because it is located at the place on Mercury which is closest to the Sun, when Mercury is farthest from the Sun.

Mercury was still a young planet when the asteroid that made Caloris Basin hit it. Mercury had not yet cooled down and become as hard as it is today. When the asteroid hit, it sent shock waves right through the planet. The shock waves collected on the opposite side of the planet from Caloris Basin. The surface of this area rose up about 3,000 feet (1,000 meters). Small ridges and hills suddenly formed in the area. Astronomers call this area "weird" or "peculiar," as it is different from the rest of Mercury.

Exploring Mercury

Mercury has been photographed through **telescopes** on Earth. These photographs show Mercury as a pale, round object with some slightly darker patches. No details can be seen.

Astronomers have taken excellent photographs of other planets using the *Hubble Space Telescope (HST)*. Mercury, however, cannot be photographed by the *Hubble Space Telescope* because it is too close to the Sun.

◀ Telescopes such as this large land optical telescope have taken pictures of Mercury, but they do not show many details.

The *Hubble Space Telescope* orbits Earth. It takes photographs of planets, stars, and other objects in space, and beams the information back to astronomers on Earth.

▲ *Mariner 10* was built in a laboratory. The people building it wore suits to protect it from dirt.

▲ *Mariner 10* launch

The only close-up photos of Mercury ever taken were made by the space probe *Mariner 10*, which visited Mercury in 1974 and 1975. The probe took more than 12,000 photographs altogether, using television cameras. The photographs were beamed back to Earth using radio waves. *Mariner 10* was launched in November 1973. It completed its work in March 1975.

Mariner 10

The space probe *Mariner 10* had two television cameras for taking pictures of Mercury, which were beamed back to Earth by a transmitter. *Mariner 10* had two antennas for receiving instructions from people on Earth. One of them was a dish and could be steered to face different directions. *Mariner 10* also had a magnetometer, an instrument that measures magnetic forces, which discovered Mercury's weak magnetic field.

Mariner 10 could make its own electricity. Its two wing-like blades were solar panels which were used to turn sunlight into electricity.

▼ *Mariner 10* in flight

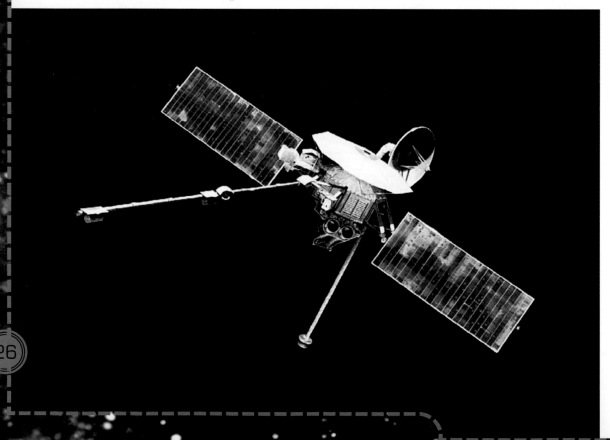

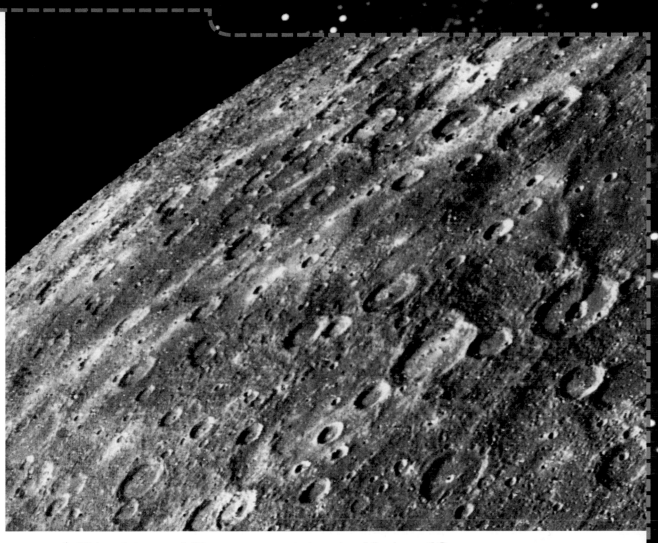

▲ This picture of Mercury was taken by *Mariner 10*

Mariner 10 reached Mercury in March 1974. It flew past, taking photographs, and then continued, flying around the Sun. The probe flew past Mercury again six months later, taking more pictures. It then orbited the Sun for another six months, before flying past Mercury for the last time. The probe is still orbiting the Sun.

Mariner 10 photographed half of Mercury's surface. This means that astronomers still do not know what the other half of Mercury looks like in detail.

Questions about Mercury

Mariner 10 collected information about less than half of Mercury's surface, so there is still a lot to learn about this planet. One day, astronomers hope to find out the answers to questions such as these:

- What is on the rest of Mercury? Are there any unusual types of craters? Do craters at the poles really have ice in them?
- What is the structure of Mercury's core?
- Why is there no iron in Mercury's crust, when it has iron in the core?
- Why is Mercury so dense? Did it lose its lightweight rocks in some violent event?
- What really happened in Mercury's past to make it the way it is today?

◀ Perhaps something crashed into the young Mercury, and broke off its outer lightweight rocks.

▲ An artist's impression of *MESSENGER*

Future Exploration

In 2004, there are plans to send another space probe to Mercury, called *MESSENGER* (short for '**Me**rcury **S**urface, **S**pace **En**vironment, **Ge**ochemistry and **R**anging' mission). The probe will reach Mercury by about 2009. The plan is to fly *MESSENGER* past Mercury twice, to make observations.

The information gathered by the instruments on board *MESSENGER* will help astronomers work out exactly why Mercury has such a high density. It will also study the crust to see what it is made of, and make measurements to see exactly what is in the thin atmosphere.

Mercury Fact Summary

Distance from Sun (average)	35,960,000 miles (57,910,000 kilometers)
Diameter (at equator)	3,030 miles (4,880 kilometers)
Mass	0.06 times Earth's mass
Density	5.43 times the density of water
Gravity	0.28 times Earth's gravity
Temperature	(day) 680 degrees Fahrenheit (360 degrees Celsius), (night) −300 degrees Fahrenheit (−180 degrees Celsius)
Rotation on axis	58.65 Earth days
Revolution	88 Earth days
Number of moons	0

Web Sites

www.psrd.hawaii.edu/Jan97/MercuryUnveiled.html
Planetary science research discoveries—Mercury unveiled

www.nineplanets.org/
The nine planets—a tour of the solar system

www.enchantedlearning.com
Enchanted Learning web site—click on "Astronomy"

stardate.org
Stargazing with the University of Texas McDonald Observatory

pds.jpl.nasa.gov/planets/welcome.htm
Images from NASA's planetary exploration program

Glossary

ancient from thousands of years ago

astronomers people who study stars, planets, and other bodies in space

atmosphere a layer of gas around a large body in space

axis an imaginary line through the middle of an object, from top to bottom

core the inside, or middle part of a planet

craters bowl-shaped holes in the ground

crust the outside layer of a planet

density a measure of how heavy something is for its size

diameter the distance across

gas a substance in which the particles are far apart, so they are not solid or liquid

gravity a force which pulls one body towards another body

lava hot liquid rock which comes from out of the ground

mantle the middle layer, underneath the crust

mass a measure of how much substance is in something

moons natural bodies which circle around planets

orbit *noun* the path a body takes when it moves around another body *verb* to travel on a path around another body in space

planet a large body which circles the Sun

pole the top or bottom of a globe

radio waves invisible rays which can carry information

revolve travel around another body

rotates spins

solar wind a stream of particles coming from the Sun

space probe a spacecraft which does not carry people

star a huge ball of glowing gas in space

telescopes instruments for making faraway objects look bigger and more detailed

Index

A

asteroids 6, 7, 14, 15, 17, 20, 22, 23
atmosphere 12–13, 15, 29, 31

C

Caloris Basin 22–3
Caloris Montes 22
comets 6, 7, 19
core 10, 11, 28, 31
craters 14–17, 18, 21, 28, 31
crust 10, 21, 28, 29, 31

D

day (Mercury) 9, 13

E

Earth 10, 11, 12, 24, 26

G

gas giants 7
gravity 8, 9, 12, 30, 31

H

halos (crater) 16
Hubble Space Telescope 24

I

ice 19, 28
iron 10, 11, 28

L

lava 15, 20–21, 31

M

magnetic field 11, 26
mantle 10, 21, 31
Mariner 10 5, 19, 25–7
Mercury (Roman god) 5
MESSENGER 29
Moon (Earth's) 10, 14, 15, 16
mountains 22
myths 4, 5, 8, 20

N

night (Mercury) 13

O

observing Mercury 4, 19, 24–7, 29
orbit (Mercury) 8–9, 31

P

plains 20–21
planets 4, 5, 6–7, 31

R

radar 19
radio waves 19, 31
rayed craters 16
revolution (Mercury) 8, 30, 31
ridges 18, 22, 23
rotation (Mercury) 9, 19, 30, 31

S

size (Mercury) 10–11, 30
soil 10
solar power 26
solar system 6–7
solar wind 12, 31
space probes 5, 19, 25–7, 29, 31
stars 4, 5, 7, 31
structure (Mercury) 10–11
Sun 4, 6, 7, 8, 9, 12, 13, 19, 23, 24, 27, 30
surface (Mercury) 14–23

T

temperature 13, 19, 21, 30
terraced craters 17

W

water 15, 19
weather 12, 15